The Greenbelt Files:

The Greenbelt Arts Festival began in 1974 when 2,000 young people with an interest in the arts, particularly rock music, gathered for a weekend celebration on a Suffolk farm. By the mid-eighties, the Festival had grown into the largest of its kind in the world, regularly attracting 25,000 for the four-day jamboree. As well as hosting the mainstage night-time rock concerts the Festival also presents a comprehensive programme of performing arts including theatre, dance, poetry, and film. A wide-ranging seminar programme, led by speakers from across the globe, examines contemporary society and cultural mores — the arts, social, political and religious issues — from a biblical perspective, and endeavours to help people to work out what being a Christian means at the end of the twentieth century.

Series Editor, Greenbelt Festival — Martin Wroe
Series Editor, MARC Europe — Tony Collins

Further information about the Greenbelt Festival, its magazine STRAIT, and its various related projects is available by writing to: Greenbelt Festivals, 11 Uxbridge Street, London W8 7TR.

D0767032

FROGS & PRINCES

For Naomi

FROGS & PRINCES

poems by MIKE STARKEY

MARC Europe
The Greenbelt Festivals

The Greenbelt Files: Series editors Martin Wroe (Greenbelt); Tony Collins (MARC Europe).

British Library Cataloguing in Publication Data
    Starkey, Mike
        Frogs and princes.
        I. Title
        821'.914   PR6069.T3/

        ISBN 0–947697–82–9

Contents

Introduction

Odd thing, poetry. For some people the mere mention of the word induces fits of yawning. It brings to mind dusty attics and school projects, old libraries and pale young men in frilly shirts.

But there's a very different kind of poetry. It's the nursery rhyme, the pop lyric, the ditty to banish washing day rain. It's the tongue-twister, the rhyme for remembering the number of days in a month, the advertising jingle you just can't get out of your head.

Once upon a time, almost all poetry was like that. It was written to be read aloud. It was written to be enjoyed. It was about heroes and dragons, frogs and princes.

The poems here are to be spoken, chanted and shouted. And (let's be honest) like nursery rhymes and tongue-twisters, a lot of them are plain daft.

Still, try looking beneath the surface and you should find a few more serious points lurking there: thoughts about the ways some people try to manipulate others, thoughts about some of the strange things people spend their lives doing.

Special thanks go to David Noble for his wonderful illustrations.

Mike Starkey

Freddie Starr Ate My Hamster
(Headline of *The Sun*
newspaper, March 1986)

Reagan's playing Star Wars
and Thatcher's buying Cruise
but fiendish Freddie's foul feast
is Britain's front-page news

Scharansky's out of Russia
Mandela's still in jail
but they're not small and furry
with a short and stubby tail

yes *The Sun* brings you the pictures
of a man who went too far
— with close-ups of the fur
between the teeth of Freddie Starr

the freedom of the press
is a democratic right
so the public needs the truth about
the unsavoury fun-size bite

The Sun says sickened Britons
are demanding stricter laws
to protect defenceless creatures
from loony lefties' jaws

now there's a building down in Wapping
where rats and ferrets roam
since *The Sun's* the only paper
where rodents feel at home

Alternative Poem

I left my London office
I left accountancy
left my bowler in a dustbin
and left the bourgeoisie
I moved to a small stone cottage
in a Welsh community
where I wear an Aran sweater
and vote Ecology

we've all got Karl Marx beards
we've all got PhDs
we've got recycled loo seats
with the badge of CND
we care for the environment
— even our pencils are lead free
so we wear our Aran sweaters
and vote Ecology

we only live off health foods
and home-grown blackberries
each morning after cold showers
we eat dry muesli
we're all keen vegetarians
we're into keeping bees
and we all wear Aran sweaters
and vote Ecology

we're all really into
conserving energy
so we sit around in armchairs
and discuss philosophy
we drink our home-brewed cider
and drive our 2CVs
and we wear our Aran sweaters
and vote Ecology

whatever politicians say
we always disagree
we're anti-vivisection
and pro-autonomy
we're into Mahatma Gandhi
and liberation for trees
and we wear our Aran sweaters
and vote Ecology

we buy our clothes from Oxfam
for good economy
we all wear pigskin sandals
and faded dungarees
our wives knit goat-hair trousers
and though they make us sneeze
they match our Aran sweaters
and we vote Ecology

I Became a Johnson's Baby

I became a Johnson's baby
and changed to Stork SB
I went in search of paradise
and invited chimps to tea

       yes I became a Johnson's baby
       now everything's OK
       I live in Marlboro Country
       and American Express pay

I got the Abbey Habit
and I'm never mean with beans
I wear my ring of confidence
when I wear my Mean Jeans

I drink my dry Martini
eat Mr Kipling's tarts
it's been a major contribution
to refreshing All Those Parts ...

I only eat my marmalade
with Gollies on the lids
and it's the wonder of Woolies
that I've got Centrally Heated Kids

I mix so well at parties
since I became a Barclay's client
but someone's after my Smarties
I think it's the Jolly Green Giant

I make someone happy
every time I use the phone
and a man in a helicopter
sits above my home

I eat my Sunshine Breakfast
and switched to Michelin
I splash my Brut all over
from a new-sized ring-pull tin

Cult Of Diana
(Press Harassment)

Diana
goddess of youth and love
our only comfort
in these troubled Times

as you ride your horses
you draw the Sun behind you

we see your name written
in every Star

and each morning the Mirror
says that you are
the fairest of all

daily
we Express our admiration

weakly
we beg you
be our Guardian

Sunbathing Poem

you'd been out in the sun all day
I said move into the shade
your skin will look like leather
but still you wouldn't be suede

Wouldn't It Be Nice

wouldn't it be nice if one Spring day
the Space Shuttle went just a little too far
and went right through a big black curtain
which surrounds the earth and it bumped
into the big light which shines through
the little holes in the curtain at night
and God said hello come and have some tea
and though scientists said
there must be some mistake
and all the philosophers said
that since God did not exist
it was pointless to discuss it
the astronauts were happy
in the big light and the
little boy sitting on
a bucket behind
the greenhouse
was
right
all
along
.
.
.

The Performance

like a verb
he knew his poetry was imperfect
and he was tense

like the moon
his face was pale
from staying up all night

like Long John Silver
at the chiropodist's
he felt only half there

like dog food
his voice
was horse

like French cigarettes
his friends
were full of useless tips

like Middlesex
the ceiling of the performance room
had Staines in the middle of it

and anyway
like Frankenstein's monster
his heart was elsewhere

but that evening
like an Eskimo with a blowtorch
he brought the house down

Church Growth

the organ's used for Mantovani
the font's been filled with coloured balls
the public sit in reclining pews
since they turned our church into a Bingo Hall

the Vicar thought it would be a way
to fill the church with needy sinners
so he bought a silver lamé suit
and calls out numbers and names of winners

it's clickety-click six six six
the pulpit's filled with things to win
and there are two fat ladies on the door
to allow the headscarved faithful in

Pilgrimage

we've travelled to the Scilly Isles and Washington DC
we've flown to Arizona and to gay Paree
we'll get away by aeroplane we'll get away by sea
as long as we can get away from VAT

we're going to a promised land where wine flows free
we're going for the Muscadet and Beaujolais and Brie
we've got a day return to Calais we'll be back in time for tea
who cares about the fares we want the Duty Free

some go to Scandinavia for the scenery
some go to France or Scotland if they want to ski
as long as we can cross a national boundary
we'll make our way to anywhere there's Duty Free

for fifty weeks a year we sit in front of the TV
with Nothing to Declare apart from what we're going to see
for fifty weeks we work out what the saving's going to be
when we make the holy journey for the Duty Free

everybody needs a littly luxury
so we're heading for the sunny side of Normandy
we'll take a seedy novel by a Conservative MP
to while away the time before the Duty Free

some go to Barcelona for the company
holding tubes of sun tan oil expectantly
we're off to Marlboro Country for a spending spree
so we'll roll up at the airport for the Duty Free

Our Father up in Heaven we declare to Thee
as we're nearing life's great customs much too rapidly
if you're having problems fixing our eternal destiny
just send us to whichever place there's Duty Free

Sweetie Pie

a question that had puzzled me
for several years was why
certain male Americans call
their girlfriends SWEETIE PIE

and when one takes his lady out
before he gets to hug her
he's usually sat for several hours
calling the poor thing SUGAR

watching programmes on TV
I always found it funny
that in the male American mind
a term that sticks is HONEY

if I were an American girl
I wouldn't feel very lucky
to have a boy who called me CHICK
like I was from Kentucky

the reason's when he's with a girl
who thinks he's trying to win her
the average male American
is thinking about his dinner

Short Love Poem for a Consumer Society

don't leave me on the shelf too long
quality goods deteriorate
grab me now while I'm still fresh
and let's go out on a 'sell-by' date

A Few Definitions

death of an Irishman	_____	Patricide
death in bed	_____	mattresside
death at the Chinese takeaway	__	sueycide
death of a salesman	_____	pesticide
death of a footballer	_____	fiveaside
death of an agnostic	_____	cantdecide

The Sweetest Girl I'd Ever Seen

I saw while looking round the shops
the sweetest girl I'd ever seen
your trousers pink with leopard spots
your hair stuck out a stiff bright green

now I'm a well-brushed kind of chap
and friends all said you weren't for me
but as we peered in Boots window
my heart was grabbed by anarchy

I knew that you could feel it too
despite friends' adolescent grins
I shyly scrutinised my shoes
you rearranged your safety pins

on afternoons we'd go for walks
your green hair blowing in the breeze
we'd sit down in the grass and talk
when you stood up you matched the trees

but one sad day you met a fellow
all my pleas were little use
his hair was orange white and yellow
violet and mauve and puce

at times like this I drop my pen
at times like this I think of you
at times like this it hurts me when
I hear you've changed your hair
to blue

Come to Marlboro Country

come to Marlboro country
and see the Marlboro folks
where the cowboys and the indians
and the animals all smokes

come to Marlboro country
where the southern ballad singers
strum on their guitars
with nicotine-stained fingers

come to Marlboro country
as you walk beneath the trees
you can hear coyotes coughing
and birds who sit and wheeze

come to Marlboro country
where the cows all smoke cigars
the milk's in packs of twenty
and is classified 'low tar'

come to Marlboro country
where they'll roll up anything
old newpapers and cotton wool
and rope and bits of string

they'll smoke old dry banana
dead grass and oily rags
I think life as a cowboy
must really be a
drag

At First It Didn't Matter

at first it didn't matter
that rather than talk with me
you preferred to watch the horror films
at night on ITV

at first it didn't matter
but it started getting scary
when your canines started growing
and your hands became all hairy

I should have understood
why on quiet evenings in
whenever I'd try to kiss you
you'd aim below my chin

and the bottles on your doorstep
— you've never really said
why one of them had milk in
but the other two were red

one evening after dinner
I thought music would be nice
so I looked through your records
— they were all by Vincent Price

I asked about your favourite group
you said you weren't selective
you liked all the major groups
— but especially Rhesus Negative

that was the point I realised
I couldn't take any more
so I fought my way past your pet bats
and creaked open your huge front door

they say you've got a new boyfriend
they say you fell for his teeth
that he buys clothes in Transylvania
and sends you flowers in wreaths

you go to all the places
we used to hang around
— the difference is with him
you both hang upside down

Psalm to the London Underground

great god of the London Underground
thou movest in mysterious ways
we have descended the abyss
and sacrificed to come into thy presence
we have read the writing on the wall
thy words have guided us
since the days of our youth
thy musicians make a joyful noise
the peoples gather from every nation
thy train fills the temple
and we wait on thee

Transformation

then I saw a new Wolverhampton
and a new Solihull
for the old ones had passed away
leaving the morning shoppers
very confused
drivers swore when the
traffic lights disappeared
letters were written
about the destruction
of historic buildings
and people said that
the light hurt their eyes
but the little old lady
from the back row of the church
got up
and ran through Handsworth
singing

Commuter Poem

man is born free
but everywhere he is in trains

Somewhere in Suburbia

she'd have had her mother's eyes
but she never had her heart
she'd have had her father's smile
but he couldn't spare the time

she could have been a radical
a twice-born evangelical
she could have been a photo
on her grandmother's wall

but the doctors get their money
and the nurses change the bedclothes
and now somewhere in suburbia
there'll be one less mouth to feed

King Herod sits in Harley Street
the land of milk and honey
while his banker's in the counting house
counting out the money

a doctor puts his raincoat on
the nurses hurry home
the Maker gets his image back
a girl drives home alone

now the doctors get their money
and the nurses change the bedclothes
and somewhere in suburbia
there'll be one less mouth to feed

High Road Low Road (a folk song)

you take the high road
and I'll take the low road
on the other hand we could have tried
that other
I still say Spaghetti Junction
was a silly way to come
to spend the week in Coventry with
your brother

we've ended up in Stourbridge twice
I'm sure I recognise
those two big cooling towers
on the right
yes maybe if we separate
we'll stand a better chance
of getting out of Birmingham
tonight

but if the road to Coventry
still proves too hard to find
then we'd better find a telephone
which functions
for you and I my true love
might never meet again
as long as we stay on
Spaghetti Junction

Arms Trade

we sell
these shells
to shell the sea shore

these shells
that we sell
shell people
I'm sure

The Princess

the Prince rode away as
the moon smiled through
the silhouettes of the enchanted
evening forest trees the air moist
and leaves underfoot
untrampled for decades

the Princess beside him
was not exactly what he
had been expecting

still things rarely are
and though she was
dripping on his cloak
he held her small green body
tightly to his
and listened as she
croaked into the
warm forest darkness

Searching for a Prince

the Princess is growing stranger since
she started searching for a Prince
the latest of her little fads
is sitting around on lily-pads

the King can never understand
(when so many Princes want her hand)
rather than wearing her best glass slippers
she comes to supper wearing flippers

still she hasn't told the Queen
why she comes in with her lips all green
and courtiers ask why she's so fond
of moonlit evenings by the pond

since the pond has only got a frog in
and it's not the perfect place to snog in

Multiplication

friend who's doing a Maths degree
there's just one thing I can't quite see
with one of me
and one of she
as you well know that's two of we
I wonder why
if we multiply
(one and one)
we'll end up
with three

Tooth Fairies

there was a whispered story
in the nursery
with Cinderella and
the tooth fairies
dreamed in the sand pit
and bright with the colours
of paint tubs

but when the news replaced stories
and teeth no longer fell out
painted pictures
faded with the sand pies
and lollipop trees

now in his armchair sometimes
he remembers Cinderella
and fingerpaints
and though he leaves his teeth
in a mug by the bedside
every night
he knows that even the tooth fairies
will never return now

Life

'the spice is going from my life'
he reflected
as thyme passed by

The Guilty Party

turn the hi-fi further up
till music fills my head
we've started on the sausage rolls
but I'm very easily led

so bring a bottle take your time
we'll talk of something arty
is that a friend? No she's my wife
and we're in a guilty party

a new girl's like a different drink
— no cause for being shocked
that neither lasts for very long
— both end up on the rocks

switch off your mind switch on a smile
and show them that you're arty
make up your face make up some tales
to tell the guilty party

your pineapple's on cocktail sticks
your mind is on the beat
you panic when the music stops
and your thoughts have lost their seat

our drinks are long our talk is small
the days are warm and arty
we're on the sunny side of life
and in a guilty party

our philosophy's like salmon paste
— it's very widely spread
since sin is like our margarine
— both of them in bred

so fill my glass with alcohol
my mind with people's laughter
and fill my thoughts with anything
... except the morning after

Thumbprints

starting
> to take down
> old walls
> and from
> the stones
> build bridges
> into a new world

running
> in new shapes
> of sunlight
> between trees
> along paths
> in places
> by the river

searching
> together
> for a world
> fresh with the
> thumbprints
> of creation

Psalm

though there are guns on the hillsides
and stones are thrown
by small children in mountain villages
though the rivers run with oil
and in the plains trenches are dug for battle
though the East Wind blows the
smoke of distant cities
and on the cedars
there is blood
still there are those who call in the wilderness
still there is a created world
which rejoices

Alligator Teeth

if you find him by the window
gazing out across the trees
then he's really shooting tigers
in a land across the seas

if he says he's spotted hippo
then it's probably the cat
ignore his green and khaki shorts
his rifle boots and hat

if he isn't on his bed
you might find him underneath
sheltering from mosquitoes
counting alligator teeth

if you meet him on the landing
then just take him back to bed
if he says he needs his rations
you can give him jam and bread

old explorers used to jungles
and nights beneath the moon
find it hard to readjust their ways
to small suburban rooms

Foot Inside Your Door

my head for sums advises you
to invest a little more
I've got your interests in my heart
and my foot inside your door

I've got a nose for bargains
no matter that you're poor
just leave your future in my hands
and my foot inside your door

so take your family savings
from the box beneath the floor
my finger's in a dozen pies
and my foot's inside your door

we'll get your mammon moving
like it's never moved before
I've got both ears to the ground
and a foot inside your door

my one desire's to ease your way
towards that distant shore
I'll put my best foot forward
and the other inside your door

on that day you'll appreciate
the money that you've saved
you'll have my coins on your eyes
and one foot
       in
          your
             grave

Nineveh

at the bottom of these high walls
the baked walls of a city
I can see dunes
long dunes to the horizon
lifting in the heat

beyond the gates in dry squares
frescoes crumble to the touch
images of vines and men
who placed their trust in sandstone
old wine stinks in the gutters
and dogs die in the dust
air is bitter
and the sweat of revelry vivid
in the music of painted rooms

I sit at the bottom of these high walls
the baked walls of a city
watching the slow approach
of a stranger
along the path through the dunes
along the path from the coast

Life's Not the Same Without You

life's not the same since you've been gone
my kitchen's full of last year's wishes
and life's too quiet without your shouts
the slam of doors the flying dishes

    life's not the same without you

the butter's dull without your hairs
there's no one here to burn the toast
to criticise my taste in clothes
and hum the songs I hate the most

    life's not the same without you

there's no one left to lose my keys
or leave my favourite LPs bent
my wallet's now become too small
for all the money left unspent

    life's not the same without you

there's no one when I watch TV
to say she wants the other channel
to squeeze the wrong end of my toothpaste
and leave her make-up on my flannel

    life's not the same without you

there's no one left to argue with
there's no one to stop talking to
and no one else in all the world
could ignore me quite the way you do

life's not the same without you

life's not the same since you've been gone
my kitchen's full of last year's wishes
and life's too quiet without your shouts
the slam of doors the flying dishes

life's not the same without you

Problem Pages

she's bypassed by the local men
her friends all seem so cruel
but problem pages understand
'frustrated of Liverpool'

she reads her weekly magazines
she's told she must be wary
lest gay neurotic impotent
her arms and legs be hairy

her eyes drift slow from page to page
her mind immersed in wine
bikinis palms and coconuts
and Paris in the Springtime

'he took her in his big strong arms
and ran his fingers through her hair'
— she's met a million newsprint men
in her terylene flowered armchair

she dreams of dancing in the street
till hunky cops arrest her
but dreams all seem to vaporise
beneath the smoke of Leicester

Hurricane

one Scandinavian evening
in the forest it started to rain
and a few little drips through the fir-cones
grew into a fierce hurricane

the wind was howling round treetops
the sun had long since ceased to shine
but I told myself not to worry
— it was God casting swirls before pine

My Inlaws Are Outlaws

I first became suspicious
although I didn't ask
when I saw your father's crowbar
his stripey shirt and mask
and then your mum objected
to being called my mother 'in law'
yes my inlaws are outlaws
and police are at our door

your brother at our wedding
wore a gun and pinstripe suit
and during the reception
he brought out a bag marked 'loot'
he took away the teacups
and then came back for more
yes my inlaws are outlaws
and police are at our door

I was invited round for tea and
you could see me lose my smile
when your mother cut a cake
and the cake contained a file
she gave us tea in teacups
I could swear I'd seen before
yes my inlaws are outlaws
and police are at our door

your sister's violin case
stays with her every day
maybe she's self-conscious
but I've never heard her play
when I asked her once she laughed at me
and said her playing's poor
yes my inlaws are outlaws
and police are at our door

we left a pub this evening
and before your glass was rinsed
two men at the next table
checked the rim for fingerprints
a man in dark sunglasses
made a note of what you wore
yes my inlaws are outlaws
and police are at our door

it's not that I don't love you
and I do like being hugged
but it is a bit offputting
when I find your wristwatch bugged
— and the body on the landing
isn't easy to ignore
yes my inlaws are outlaws
and police are at our door

Video Nasties

on evenings in (as I record)
we'd sit together and televise
me with my remote control
you with your beautiful big square eyes

my life had started off as blank
now things were moving forward fast
I'd hold your picture in its frame
and hope the future wouldn't contrast

but coming in from work one day
as I was starting to unwind
the bad reception I received
showed you'd had a change of mind

you looked me squarely in the eye
you cleared your voice and chose your tone
and said you felt that our romance
was starting to grow monochrome

you said we'd have to wind it up
the final credits were in sight
so then I turned my volume up
and said things weren't so black and white

all the same you packed your case
— you've been away for several weeks
and no amount of self-control
can adjust the colour in my cheeks

I take long walks to clear my head
– to make my feelings less affected
but when I stop or pause a while
I still can't help but feel ejected

Sunday

Sunday morning over Bolton
and
in the launderette
the belles
were wringing out

Get On Down

HEY THERE BABE NOW GET ON DOWN
HIP HIP HOP AND ROUND AND ROUND
LET'S SHAKE OUR FUNK AND MOVE OUR FEET
DIG THAT RHYTHM GRAB THAT BEAT
MOVING THERE AND MOVING HERE
HIPPING OUTA THIS ATMOSPHERE
JUMP ON IN AND CHECK IT OUT
I'LL SHOW YOU WHAT IT'S ALL ABOUT
GETTING DOWN LET'S START TO MOVE
HOP AND DIP WE GOT THE GROOVE
BOP BOP BOP AND NEVER DROPPIN'
BOOGIE TIME AIN'T NEVER STOPPIN'

baby I love to be with you
my parents just don't understand me

If Music Be the Food of Love ...

what you said to me in the bar
made my knees quaver
and my emotions
zither
in fact
I could hardly
breve
I do hope
you aren't a
lyre

Botanical Gardens

just for an hour
we were explorers
cutting our path through
the leaves of the glasshouses
along untrodden concrete
investigating new thermostats
and uncharted doors
classifying sprinkler systems
in search of the source
of the tapwater
evangelising
previously unreached cacti
and holding hands
as we sneaked past
bands of natives
their cameras ready
to shoot on sight

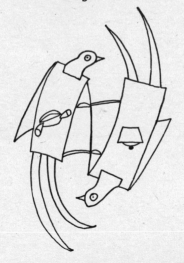

The Man From Mars

the chocolates that the lady loves
were left inside her room to tempt her
she swallowed all of his dark lies
since he'd appealed to her soft centre

      he's a sweet-talking guy
      who stands in bars
      you'll know when you've been tempted by
      the Man from Mars

he'll promise you the galaxy
and try to lead your will astray
with promises of bumper packs
of endless work and rest and play

you'll always find him well wrapped-up
and in his paper-thin disguise
he'll drive you in his Mini Rolls
and say he thinks that you're fun-size

a chocolate finger beckons to
the innocent victims that he picks
he leaves his mark upon their teeth
and on their forehead 'Twix Twix Twix'

      he's a sweet-talking guy
      who stands in bars
      a tempter with a company car
      a salesman versed in la-di-da
      an ad-man with a big cigar

      you'll know when you've been tempted by
      the Man from Mars

Small Ads

I must admit I didn't find it
in the slightest bit surprising
that when I asked about your job
you said you were in advertising

you'd put some small ads in the papers
to try to turn my thoughts to you
you gave me bags that had your name on
and pasted posters in my loo

you'd told me after seven days
you'd found out all you need to know
— my body needed servicing
but my fuel consumption seemed quite low

then on the day I asked you out
you said that in selecting you
I'd won a set of tasteless mugs
and a holiday in Spain for two

I said you set my heart aflame
I longed to see how you'd react
you said my innards contravened
the English Trades Descriptions Act

so when at last I took the plunge
and asked you if you'd marry me
you made me give you a receipt
and sign a ten-year guarantee

The Boy Who Follows My Sister Round

there's a boy who follows my sister round
and while he tries to please her
my sister feels about him the way
Boadicea felt about Caesar

her amorous desires are such
that it won't come as a shock
to learn that she needs him the way
Covent Garden needs punk rock

he smiles at her in a meaningful way
but still she gives him looks
which could be those of snails and frogs
whenever they see French cooks

he writes romantic poetry
and gives it to her sweetly
but my sister reads his verses like
the Pope reads Dennis Wheatley

his presents are extravagant
he's always sending roses
but she longs for his presents like
a rabbit for myxomatosis

So as I follow you around
I'm sure that you'd agree
my sister's as involved with him
as you want to be with me

Problem

queueing
in the USSR
is a problem
of long standing

Shampoo

when hair falls out each time you brush it
and you try to stick it back with glue
when friends leave toupees on your doorstep
I think you'd better change shampoo

when you find hairs on settees and chairs
and the moulting's not the dog but you
when colleagues (like your ends) all split
I think you'd better change shampoo

when waking up you feel light headed
and your mirror tells you that it's true
your pillow looks like a bearskin rug
I think you'd better change shampoo

when she rests her head by yours
and whispers though she's fond of you
she likes her suitors to be hirsuter
I think you'd better change shampoo

when you look at recent photos
and realise what your friends all knew
your airy areas were once much hairier
I think you'd better change shampoo

so as you sit beside your window
looking out across the view
your hopes your hair all falling through
you've cancelled your holiday in Corfu
you're going to stay at home in lieu
you think of how your hair once grew
you just don't know what you can do
the trees are bare your head is too
after all you're only twenty-two
I think you'd better change shampoo

Godot
(In response to Samuel Beckett's play)

the audience were all well dressed
and sat contentedly depressed
by the pointlessness of the modern age
when suddenly Godot walked on stage

the jawbones of the actors dropped
when suddenly their waiting stopped
the prompt girl tried to find the page
where Godot's meant to walk on stage

the usherette could sense disaster
when the manager ran past her
working out the extra wage
now that Godot had walked on stage

the critics said they found it hard
to take such joy in avant garde
it spoilt the spirit of the age
to witness Godot walk on stage

the audience agreed that it would wreck it
to have a happy end in Beckett
and so they all walked out in rage
when they saw Godot walk on stage

but a lady in a crocheted shawl
sitting in the lower stalls
leaned and whispered to her friend
that she DID like plays with a happy end

Two Old Ladies

The two old ladies were in total agreement;
the trouble with young people was not only
that they made themselves look ridiculous:
dyeing their hair in absurd colours and
wearing tasteless clothing: but that they
wasted so much time and were so rude
to others.

The two old ladies were glad that they had
agreed for once; they pulled on their
simulated fur coats and hurried off to spend
the rest of the day at the hairdresser's;
he was a nice man, despite his wife, and
he always did such a good job with their
pink rinses.

Walking to Work

end of apple time
and the morning early as milk bottles

sunlight on the railway bridge
warm condensation winking
on the café windows

a small Chinese man in a furry hat
and a big coat
is watching the trains

end of apple time
walking to work
thinking about you
blackberries
and still autumn woods

as angels chuckle
beyond the tiled rooftops
of Mill Road

Mr Adam

tell me Mr Adam
how does your garden grow
— with warning bells and nuclear shells
and Eve on video

    with pinstripe yuppie businessmen
    a-standing in a row
    with hamburgers and horoscopes
    and all-night movie shows

    with love in plain brown envelopes
    from people you don't know
    with grasping TV preachers
    seeking profits here below

so tell me Mr Adam
how does your garden grow
— with warning bells and nuclear shells
and Eve on video

    with concrete-covered landscapes
    where toxic rivers flow
    as girls and boys come out to play
    beneath a neon glow

    with Cain paid for talking
    in a TV studio
    where they play slow-motion replays
    and you watch them blow by blow

so tell me Mr Adam
how does your garden grow
— with all the seeds you planted
a long long time ago

Mike Starkey

Poet and journalist Mike Starkey was born in Cheshire in 1963. He started writing and performing poems as a student at Oxford University and has published two earlier booklets of poetry, *Inlaws and Outlaws* and *Poems and Trees*. The best of these two volumes is included in *Frogs and Princes*. He is well known as a performer at concert venues all over Britain.

Mike spent a year as presenter of a nightly programme on French radio. He recently married Naomi and they live in Cambridge.

Concerts

In his past attempts at bringing poetry to the masses, Mike Starkey has considered offering the following services:

*BARDOGRAM — A poetic equivalent of the 'Kissagram'. An unsuspecting individual is approached by a disguised poet. The poet suddenly reveals his true identity and humiliates the victim by giving a half hour poetry reading.

*ROMANTIC — The poet wears a frilly shirt and tiptoes around your garden, looking at the flowers with a tempestuous expression in his eyes. Furrows his brow at regular intervals. Payment at an hourly rate.

*BALLADEER — The poet sits in your lounge on long winter evenings, waving his arms and declaiming his verse in a passionate voice. Beard optional. Toast and hot chocolate must be provided.

*LAUREATE — The poet is paid to write about dead sheep.

Due to the notable absence of public enthusiasm for these earlier strategies, Mike Starkey is now offering himself for performances at your local youth club/school/pop concert/church/pub/coffee bar/literary society.

He can be contacted at:

P.O. Box 32
Cambridge
CB1 3PF

What Is World Vision?

World Vision is a major Christian relief and development agency, founded over 35 years ago. World Vision now helps the hungry, the homeless, the sick and the poor in over 80 countries worldwide.

World Vision is international, interdenominational and has no political affiliation, working wherever possible through local churches and community leaders in close co-operation with the United Nations and other international relief agencies.

Childcare sponsorship is an important part of World Vision's Christian work. Over 400,000 children are currently being cared for in over 3,500 projects.

Sponsors in Europe and around the world are helping thousands of needy children by supplying food, clothing, medical care and schooling. These children usually live with their families although some are in schools or homes. Development and training are usually offered to the communities where the sponsored children live so that whole families can become self-reliant.

World Vision is able to respond with immediate and appropriate relief in crisis situations such as famines, floods, earthquakes and wars. Hundreds of thousands have been saved in Africa through feeding and medical centres. Other projects include cyclone relief for Bangladesh, relief work in Lebanon and medical assistance for Kampuchea.

Over 500 community development projects in 50 countries are helping people to help themselves towards a healthier and more stable future. These projects include agricultural and vocational training, improvements in health care and nutrition (especially for mothers and babies), instruction in hygiene, literacy classes for children and adults, development of clean water supplies and village leadership training.

World Vision's approach to aid is integrated in the sense that we believe in helping every aspect of a person's life and needs. We also help Christian leaders throughout the world to become more effective in their ministry and assist local churches in many lands with their work.

If you would like more information about the work of World Vision, please contact one of the offices listed below:

World Vision of Britain
Dychurch House
8 Abington Street
Northampton
NN1 2AJ, United Kingdom
Tel: 0604 22964

World Vision of Australia
Box 399–C, G P O
Melbourne, 3001 Victoria
Australia
Tel: 3 699 8522

World Vision Deutschland
Postfach 1848
Adenauerallee 32
D–6370 Oberursel
West Germany
Tel: 6171 56074/5/6/7

World Vision International
Christliches Hilfswerk
Mariahilferstr 10/10
A-1070 Wien
Austria
Tel: 222–961 333/366

World Vision International
Christliches Hilfswerk
Badenserstr 87
CH-8004 Zürich
Switzerland
Tel: 1–241 7222

World Vision of Ireland
17 Percy Place
Dublin 4
Eire
Tel: 01 606 058

World Vision Singapore
Maxwell Rd
PO Box 2878
Singapore 9048
Tel: 224–8037/7419

Suomen World Vision
Kalevankatu 14 C 13
00100 Helsinki 10
Finland
Tel: 90 603422

World Vision of New Zealand
PO Box 1923
Auckland
New Zealand
Tel: 9 770 879

Stichting World
Vision Nederland
Postbus 818
3800 AV Amersfoort
The Netherlands
Tel: 33 10041

World Vision Canada
6630 Turner Valley Rd
Mississauga, Ontario
Canada L5N 2S4
Tel: 416 821 3030

World Vision United States
919 West Huntington Drive
Monrovia
CA 91016
USA
Tel: 818 303 8811

World Vision of Hong Kong
PO Box 98580
Tsim Sha Tsui Post Office
Kowloon
Hong Kong
Tel: 3–7221634

The Publisher

MARC Europe is an integral part of World Vision, an international Christian humanitarian organisation. MARC's object is to assist Christian leaders with factual information surveys, management skills, strategic planning and other tools for evangelism. MARC Europe also publishes and distributes related books on matters of mission, church growth, management, spiritual maturity and other topics.

IMAGINATION
Embracing a Theology of Wonder
by Cheryl Forbes

First in the new series co-published by MARC Europe and the Greenbelt Arts Festival, exploring contemporary issues from a Christian perspective.

Imagination is the God-given ability of seeing life freshly. It helps us fill our lives with meaning. It is an energetic discipline, fuelled by the example of Christ himself. Cheryl Forbes, author of *The Religion of Power*, shows imagination at work in many different ways and many different people. Imagination, she shows us, empowers not only musicians and artists, but scientists, housewives, students, and office workers.

Cheryl Forbes teaches at Calvin College in Michigan. She has worked for both *Christianity Today* and Zondervan Publishing House.

Of this latest book *Publishers Weekly* said that it shows us how 'imagination can help awaken the transforming power of Christ.'

Co-published with the Greenbelt Arts Festival

192pp   £2.50

DARK GLASSES
Sex, poetry, the media and quite a bit else
Edited by Steve Shaw and Sue Plater

Another Greenbelt Files book —

Why should the thorny subjects so often be swept under the carpet? Isn't it time the Church started talking, thinking, and acting on contemporary issues?

Steve Shaw and Sue Plater have collected a series of essays with questions and responses for discussion starters. Homosexuality, the theatre, materialism, feminism, pornography, rock music — all these and many other subjects come under thoughtful scrutiny by a well known panel of writers including Pip Wilson, Martin Wroe, Nigel Forde, Stewart Henderson and Viv Faull.

An indispensable book for youth and their leaders, for new Christians, for any who are asking questions.

Co-published with the Greenbelt Arts Festival.

192pp   £3.95

ROLLING IN THE AISLES
by Murray Watts

Tired of the same old sermon illustrations and after-dinner jokes at Christian gatherings? This book is a must for anyone looking for the telling anecdote or the pithy summary to a preaching point.

Illuminating, poignant, and provocative, the short tales in *Rolling in the Aisles* makes our sides ache with laughter. But the humour doesn't stop there; it probes more deeply so that we see the truth about ourselves.

Murray Watts is a playwright and one of the founding directors of the Riding Lights Theatre Company, award winners at the Edinburgh Fringe Festival and famous for a unique blend of comic and serious material. He is the author of several books and many plays, editor of *Laughter in Heaven*, and major contributor to *Playing with Fire*.

Front cover art by Norman Stone.

Foreword by Sir Harry Secombe.

A royalty from every book sold goes to the work of the Children's Society.

Co-published with the Children's Society

128pp   £2.25

ONE STAGE FURTHER
by Nigel Forde

In the tradition of Riding Lights Theatre Company's usual wit and polish, *One Stage Further* provides more entertaining and fast-moving sketches for performance by church groups and other amateur companies. Here Nigel Forde has written sixteen sketches and one full-length play, *Angel at Large*, to make us laugh, to make us think, and to make us want to change.

Doctor: It sounds as if you'd have done better to go to your dentist rather than come to me.
Rector: To a dentist?
Doctor: I think so, yes. I think what you've got there is a hollow truth. (Peers.) Just as I thought. There's a large truth here with a great, gaping hole in it. Too many sugary choruses...

'A collection of sketches on spiritual and moral themes that leap off the page with verve and wit.'
James Fox in his _Preface_

160pp   £2.25

PLAYING WITH FIRE
Edited by Paul Burbridge

Five Stageplays from the Riding Lights Theatre Company

Wherever the Riding Lights Theatre Company takes its plays, the cast is greeted with high acclaim. Paul Burbridge's selection of plays in this book will prove no exception.

Catwalk — Murray Watts portrays a prisoner of conscience in a Russian psychiatric hospital. Is he or is he not mad because of his faith?

St John's Gospel — Murray Watts' adaptation of the Gospel of John brings fresh insight to the familiar words.

A Winter's Tale — Nigel Forde travels with the Three Magi to show us the hilarious consequences of the gifts brought for the Christ Child — when the Magi meet the local customs officers and the camel has a mind of its own.

Promise — Andrew Goreing uncovers the anguish of a woman suffering from multiple sclerosis who seeks healing.

A Gentleman's Agreement — Murray Watts leads us through the hilarious escapades and misunderstandings of a group of undergraduates on the eve of their graduation.

Five full-length plays that will entertain, challenge and provoke.

224pp   £3.95

THEATRECRAFT
by Nigel Forde

At last a superbly written insight into the world of drama takes centre stage!

Theatrecraft is the perfect book to guide the aspiring drama group, while providing added insights for those more experienced in drama production. Nigel Forde, writing from 20 years' experience as a professional actor, playwright and producer, places a Christian perspective on the theory and practice of drama.

Theatrecraft covers acting, stagecraft, directing, writing and stage management, as well as discussing the theology of the theatre and the role of the artist. Nigel Forde writes with humour and vitality; *Theatrecraft* is a superbly written, clear-thinking introduction to the world of drama.

Nigel Forde is a director of the Riding Lights Theatre Company in York. He is also resident poet of BBC Radio 4's 'Midweek' programme and a regular writer for 'Start the Week'. He was a finalist in last year's Observer/Arvon International Poetry Competition.

'A "must" for all church drama groups'
Church of England Newspaper

192pp £2.25

THE RELIGION OF POWER
by Cheryl Forbes

An examination of the insidious use and abuse of power within the Christian Church. What power games do we unconsciously play to manipulate others? How can we truly reflect the humility and sincere love of Christ?

Cheryl Forbes probes with her incisive intelligence into these deep questions. She shows us that power and the quest for power are intoxicating. We come away from this book changed people.

'Recommended to all'
Buzz

176pp £1.95